SIMPLE
STRATEGIES
TO SUCCESS

Adriana **Cecere**

Global Leaders in Consulting

Adriana Cecere
Consulting Australia

Founder, Consulting Australia

There are many paths to becoming one of Consulting's Global Leaders in Consulting, and for Adriana Cecere, that journey started on a farm. She credits her "humble beginnings," being raised by her wonderful Italian parents, grandparents and brother on a farm, to her career success. Also, she is a very curious person, by nature. This combination found her owning her first business at just 17 years old.

"I developed this enterprise into a multi-award business franchise over 19 years. This was my real life MBA," she says. "While setting up other businesses before Consulting Australia, the biggest factor to my success would be my hunger to continually improve—clients' experience, my business, my self and the greater community."

Today, Cecere runs Consulting Australia, an Alignment and Growth consultancy for leaders, based in Sydney. The methodology has been proven, developed by modeling strategies she used whilst starting, developing, and selling more than ten companies over the past two decades. Cecere is also the author of an Amazon best-selling book, *Game Changers: Entrepreneurs Leading Change*.

She works with Business and Industry Leaders on their development and Business Transformation. As President and Chair to the Board of AusCam Freedom Project, she also strengthens the work of charities to empower adolescent girls from impoverished communities gain an education.

As to what she's most proud of in her career and she'll say developing a new, innovative online business program to help business leaders and professionals abroad, and in remote regions to gain clarity, skills and learnings at an affordable price point. She also launched, grew and sold more than ten self-owned, award-winning businesses over the past two decades. She is also about to publish her second book.

Cecere says an injury in 2008 changed her career path and business direction overnight, but the challenging experience turned out to be a highlight. "Through the experience my new found empathy and learning shaped me into a better business women and leader," she says. "Business Leaders, Boards and organizations then started to approach me." Out of that, Consulting Australia was born.

"I thrive on seeing businesses and people flourish. Consulting is rewarding as it allows us to nurture business leaders and help their business align, transform, develop and grow," Cecere says. "Watching the full cycle can be challenging yet very rewarding."

To be named a Global Leader is an "absolute honor," she says. "This recognition is the reflection of all the years of hard work put into every client project. The team is super proud. This is also the result of trust that my clients have put into Consulting Australia, allowing me to advise and mentor them and obtaining positive outcomes."

Q&A: What motivates you to excel?

Cecere: "I am purpose driven. My husband, family and team motivate me to excel. Especially my children aged 4 years and 2 years, as a mother I want them to be grounded and educate them to value perseverance and commitment."

Published in *Consulting Magazine*, New York, 18 January 2018.

I have had the delight of working with Adriana for several years now.

She has transformed from traditional business consulting to be known as The Back-Pocket CEO.

Adriana provides high quality, innovative and successful support that delivers results. She has dared to be different in a traditional environment and is reaping the rewards.

STEVE BROSSMAN
FOUNDER AND CEO
THE AUTHORITY FACTOR

"Admirable talent and poise which can only be achieved using the heart and mind in unison. A good balance of values, beliefs and ethics – complimented with a wealth of tenacity, experience and generosity is how I see and feel about Adriana Cecere."

ZOE CAMPBELL
FOUNDER OF COMPUTER COACH AUSTRALIA
ACTRESS

"Adriana's excellent book contains real wisdom and practical advice for setting and achieving one's goals and for leading a fulfilling life.

Adriana puts into practice what she advocates in her book by volunteering her time to help us at The Buttery to fulfil our mission.

The Buttery is a charity working to help teenagers and adults manage mental health and substance misuse issues.

We are most grateful to Adriana for her contribution."

CHRIS BENAUD
DEVELOPMENT MANAGER
THE BUTTERY
WWW.BUTTERY.ORG.AU

"Adriana's experience and ability to understand my vision enables me to build a plan of action, that considers my customers, staff, and own personal goals.

Adriana seamlessly applies her knowledge not only to the benefit of my business, but to me as a business owner.

My team and I enjoy our in-depth discussions and treat every meeting as an opportunity to grow."

ALAN MERCIECA
GENERAL MANAGER
MERMED AUSTRALIA

SIMPLE
STRATEGIES
TO SUCCESS

28 DAYS WITH

Adriana **Cecere**

The BackPocket CEO

Photos by Jom
Cover Design by Zak
Editing by Jacki Ferro

ISBN 978-1-925732-50-4

This book is dedicated to my husband Mark who encourages me to follow my dreams and embrace even the wildest business ideas.

And to our children Pia Olivia and Alessandro James, who inspire and ground me, keeping things simple and meaningful in line with life's deeper purpose.

To my parents for their support and example, in particular their beautiful and humble approach to life. Thank you for allowing me to
spread my wings and fly.

This book is also dedicated to you, the reader, and to my wonderful clients and followers whose praise and gratitude gives me courage, and helps fuel my passion to continue. Please enjoy this handbook. I hope it brings you further clarity, confidence and purpose in your unique journey, and makes a positive difference as balanced leaders driving successful, purpose-built businesses.

Throughout the writing process, I have been mindful to build this as a handbook, so you have great information to refer back to quickly to get the most out of a purpose-filled, successful business and life.

A Special Gift for You

For purchasing *Simple Strategies to Success*, you receive a Lifetime Membership with a personalised log-in to the Academy of Business where you can access up-to-date business tools and templates, which appear in the handbook, plus many more.

Email me at adriana@consultingaustralia.com.au to gain your login details.

I would love to hear from you with any feedback and comments.

A donation from each book sold at the launch was donated to The Buttery Foundation.

THE BUTTERY

http:// www.buttery.org.au/the-buttery-private-3/
https://www.buttery.org.au

A percentage of ongoing book sales will be donated to The Buttery Foundation and Children's Charities.

"It always seems impossible until it's done"

NELSON MANDELA

(C. 1918–2013)

PRESIDENT OF SOUTH AFRICA 1994–1999

REVOLUTIONARY POLITICAL LEADER

ABOUT THE AUTHOR

 **A**driana Cecere runs an alignment and growth consultancy for business leaders based in Sydney, Australia. Her methodology has been proven; developed by modelling strategies that Adriana used while starting, developing and selling more than ten companies over the past two decades.

The programs have depth and are outcome-focused—bespoke and unlimited.

Adriana's extensive experience and seasoned skills allow her to quickly identify both core issues in a business, and the client's strengths and weaknesses. Adriana's approach helps clients improve empathy and measure accountability. High-achieving and successful leaders, board members, industry professionals and entrepreneurs call on Adriana for her expertise.

Labeled *The BackPocket CEO*, Adriana has written the Amazon #1 best-selling book, *Game Changers: Entrepreneurs Leading Change*. She works with business and industry leaders on their development, business alignment, transformation and growth.

Adriana's big picture is to help leaders across the globe make a difference in their lives, their businesses, and the greater community.

As President and Chair AusCam Freedom Project, Adriana also strengthens the work of charities that empower adolescent girls from impoverished communities to obtain an education. As an Advisory Committee member of The Buttery Foundation, she supports and promotes development of their programs, designed to rebuild and empower people recovering from substance abuse.

NOTE TO YOU FROM ADRIANA

Welcome to *Simple Strategies to Success*. We are about to embark on your unique 28-day journey where you will discover then develop and align different elements of your life before adopting new focuses to achieve better results in your business, professional, and personal life.

Before we begin, take a moment to think of what you want your business to look like.

What do you really need? What changes must you make to get there?

You may be a chief executive officer, president of a board, internationally recognised sportsperson, industry leader, business owner or entrepreneur starting out. Think about the type of professional you want to be recognised as, what you want to achieve as a professional, who you want to become, and how this can translate into reality and align with your personal life and goals.

Don't worry if you don't know all the answers at this point, just be mindful that shortly you will take a deep dive into yourself where you will have to think about and incorporate all three elements of your life as one person. We will work on the "whole you" to build your business as sustainable and one that is aligned with your career and personal, long-term success.

Here's to you and your success—purpose-driven and fueled with positive energy and abundance.

I am honored and excited to be a part of this journey with you.

Enjoy!

ADRIANA CECERE

The BackPocket CEO

INTRODUCTION

This book is all about you, helping you keep it simple and gain clarity while gaining confidence that is meaningful, purpose-driven and transformational. As my clients know, I have strong beliefs in the power of living life that's aligned and balanced both personally and professionally to sustain long-term commercial success.

"Plan, prepare, deliver quality results on time"

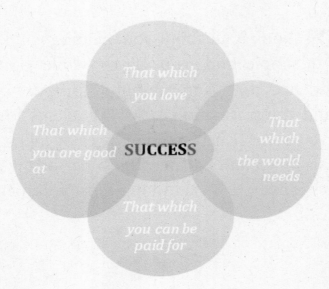

PREPARATION

When our personal, professional and business goals are aligned with purpose and an action plan, we achieve our goals with more ease. Even when the odds are against us, the solutions to overcome these obstacles are more easily identified and then chosen, because we are traveling through life mindful of our purpose-aligned goals, which we own.

Life's journey will get challenging at times, but with this established foundational belief, no mountain is too big to stop us.

My focus is for optimal living in all areas of my life. Being a wife, mum, and business-woman, my first and foremost business is me.

If I am strong and focused, I can retain clarity to lead by example and maintain momentum towards positive goals in my personal life, professional schedule, and business growth.

If you have flown on an airplane once or twice before, you will recall that, before takeoff, flight stewards usually announce something to the effect of, "In case of an emergency, an oxygen mask will drop from above. Place it over your mouth first then take other masks to help children". They instruct adults to place it over their mouths first before assisting children and others. This is a powerful analogy, which I was lucky to hear at a young age, and it resonated.

Coming from a traditional Italian family with great family values, I was not taught elements taken from this analogy as part of my upbringing.

As in many traditional cultures and communities, Italian families often groom their youngsters, especially girls, to believe they need to put themselves last, and everything and everybody else first. After this analogy resonated, I studied other successful people, especially women, and realized that this belief doesn't serve us well. That said, I believe that by retaining a portion of being confidently selfless has contributed to my business success and ability as a mother and wife. It is imperative, however, to be mindful and prioritize when to apply the brakes, choose which hats to wear when, and include time in your schedule for sharpening your tools, filling your emotional and relationship bank, and being there for family and friends while driving towards your goals.

Don't be a people-pleaser—make choices that support and align with your chosen direction and goals. If this focus is new to you, it will feel extremely odd at first, but once you start to make this belief shift, doors will open, moving you closer to your goals. When you master the right combination of selflessness and managing your time aligned with your life's purpose and goals, you will feel more confident with this newfound clarity and direction. You will become a person with a strong identity, you will communicate more easily with your colleagues, staff and clients, and you will own your goals and take appropriate action. Your business will start making its way to the next level and you will confidently drive on to the next milestone of your clear plan.

What stops most people is guilt.

Be mindful of not being able to break off old habits set by past beliefs or pressures from others as you prepare for your 28-day journey.

My grandfather, Nonno Michaele, used to tell us as youngsters, "You need to choose friends that are people you want to become." It's okay to have lifelong friends you see from time to time who have different goals, as long as you have a mutual respect for and understanding of one another's direction in life.

Similarly, it is important to let go of guilt and not feel bad, if you want to achieve greater goals. You must respectfully select what you choose to focus your time on. Be kind to yourself—love yourself enough to take care of your physical and mental health, and your emotional and spiritual well-being. Embrace self-love as a foundational ingredient as you dive into what you really want to discover: your goals aligned with purpose to live the life you want and deserve.

If you have not yet adopted this foundational mindset, commit to yourself now to make this shift so we can get through the next 28 days together, making good choices and taking the actions necessary to make a positive difference to your future.

Most people I work with are smart, successful people who are motivated and astute at reaching their goals. I have found they don't need to be told what to do or how to be motivated. They need things simplified, however, so that they can return to their purpose without the clutter. My strategies allow them to gain clarity and refocus on their chosen purpose in both their personal and professional lives. Through this handbook, we will work together with tools and a measured, accountable action plan to help you become the best version of yourself and develop your business.

My approach is powerful—it lays a strong foundation for success in business, and provides satisfaction, both personally and professionally.

Remember to nurture your development and take care of you, so that you can give to your staff and business, enabling growth and scale. Then give back to your family a better version of yourself, which they all deserve.

"Give the best, be the best, then the best will come"

Adriana Cecere

CONTENTS

1   DISCOVERY   1
    The Power of Clarity   24

2   DESIGN AND ALIGN   41
    Strategic Planning   59

3   TRANSFORMATION   65
    Successful Transformation   82

4   OPTIMIZATION   103
    For Optimization   122

CHAPTER ONE
DISCOVERY
DAYS 1 – 7

"If you want to live a happy life, tie it to a goal, not people or objects"

ALBERT EINSTEIN
(c. 1879–1955)
THEORETICAL PHYSICIST

DISCOVERY TEACHINGS

In this first step, we will examine in detail what you want to achieve in your business, professional and personal life. Be open-minded to possibilities, discount any limiting beliefs, and internalize to discover your deepest purpose, what your drive is, and what you want your life to look like.

YOUR PERSONAL GOALS

We will start with your personal goals.

On this thought, consider your family, what they need in the short and long term and what you need to do to support them.

Do you have enough time in your day to spend with family and friends?

Are your finances adequate to support your family's needs?

Do you have enough time for yourself to reflect, revitalize, dream and plan?

YOUR PROFESSIONAL GOALS

Let's turn to your professional goals.

What skills do you need to gain and develop to perform better at your job?

Who do you need to develop or employ around you to support you to deliver your professional aspirations? Is it a coach? Do you need to go back to study? Should you choose a mentor? Do you need a personal assistant to conduct important scheduling and administrative tasks, so that you are free to create and focus on your strategic position and long-term vision?

Are you connected within your professional network? Do you support and help your network?

Do you need to study any courses to develop?

Do you allow time to read?

Do you allow time to be present?

Do you have a mentor or coach or someone you can call on as an objective soundboard who keeps you accountable? If you are a business professional or professional sports athlete (Sports Star), is your mindset optimized to perform at your best?

YOUR BUSINESS OBJECTIVES

Now examine your business objectives.

Is your business working for you? Returning a profit? Making the money you envisage? Do you have a business plan? Goals? Does your business deliver to clients their expectations? How do you rate your level of client service? Are your business goals aligned with your succession plan? Do you have a succession plan? If you are the senior leader of your business, as CEO or President, does the organizational structure reflect what both the business and you need to take the business to the next level and reach its next milestone? Does your business support an environmentally friendly future?

If you are the founder of your business, are your professional and personal goals aligned with the business?

Phew! A lot of work to do and many things to consider. But don't be alarmed, I have summarized this into a palatable worksheet below for you to digest and work through over the next seven days.

Before we start, one important question to ask yourself is this:

Does good synergy exist among your personal, professional, and business goals?

I recall a turning point in my life when I knew that I needed to dig deeper to identify what I wanted my next phase of life to look like. First, I reflected on all I had achieved. Next, I categorized what I enjoyed and wanted to take with me to my next phase. I identified too what I didn't enjoy or didn't want to take into my next phase of business. I then added what I wanted to achieve and how I wanted my life to look, and painted that clear picture into a vision. This process of elimination was invaluable; it provided me great clarity and helped to crystalize what I wanted my future to look like, including the vision for my business.

Over the next seven days, complete the following worksheet and start thinking about what you need to do to achieve these goals for your business and lifestyle.

At the start of each day, get into the right state of mind and work through the worksheet. The following morning, before you start your day, revise your answers with a different perspective and hone your goals, taking ownership of them.

Each day, take five minutes to visualize yourself and business already achieving your goals.

Create a bright, strong picture in your mind of yourself and your family, living the life you envision for them. Work through what your day will look like, think about and visualize how your work and business will be and what your workplace will look like. Think about and bring into the picture those who will be working for you, and bring into this picture too your new coach and mentor. Visualize the blissful feeling you will have in every cell of your body when you go to bed each night feeling the peace and satisfaction after your day. Each day, feel the gears shifting as your life and business start to take shape.

During your meditation, fast-forward ten years from now—dream, feel, smell and see what you will be doing; imagine who you will be around and what your business looks like and how cash flow is now positive. Think about your health, fitness and mental well-being in a positive, strong, clear and relaxed state. Keep focus on this picture.

Do this every day.

As you process this daily ritual, if you feel something is unaligned with your picture, zone in on it. Ask yourself why you are feeling this way. Why are you feeling this block?

If an experience from childhood or your upbringing has shaped this belief, it may result in this block stopping you from getting past this level—don't dismiss this block. If you feel it, you must stop, reflect and internalize why and when this limiting belief began.

Everyone has a story, something that has happened to them or something somebody said to them or in a tone, which has affected that individual in their future years. The beauty is, you are reading this book, and have reached this point, so you are open to change and self-improvement.

Acknowledge this feeling and block and realize that it is not aligned with you now; if it was, it would not create in you this negative feeling.

One way to eliminate this block with ease is to read your goals each day. Then, go through the daily ritual of closing your eyes and visualize reaching your goals— see how your life and business will look, feel and smell tomorrow, and in three, six, and twelve months. Then picture your life in three, five, and ten years' time—feeling so good and aligned with your greater purpose. If you get that negative feeling and block, or come across a person in your future whom you previously allowed to create a roadblock, zone into that situation and throw it up in the air. Plant your feet firmly on the ground, feet a little apart. Let your shoulders relax, and hang your hands and fingers relaxed and confidently beside your hips. Relax your neck and imagine an angel pulling up your ears. Let your chin relax and remain poised.

Look up at the person or situation or feeling soaring up and up, until it almost disappears, watch it move fast now behind you as it disappears.

Keep breathing slow, deep breaths. Now, as you can still almost only just see it, hand it over to a greater being. Let it soar faster and faster up higher into the sky and back further behind you into the past.

Allow yourself to let go of this.

Now visualize your bright picture again, free from resistance with newfound clarity and confidence.

Open your eyes.

Each morning, follow the same ritual. Feel the gears shifting as you simply align with your goals, allowing for growth and strategic transformation. Then allow for optimization and success to filter through each area of your life, achieving your purpose-driven personal, professional and business goals.

"*Obstacles are things a person sees when he takes his eyes off his goal*"

E. Joseph Cossman
(c. 1918–2002)
Author
Businessman

Introduce time for self-care each day. The power of taking care of yourself and giving back to you is severely underestimated. If you don't take care of yourself first, how can you care for your family, nurture relationships, or give your business the attention and care it needs to flourish?

From today, put yourself first. Keeping your own tank full will take self-control and focus, but it is imperative to you becoming the best you can be and helping to develop your business to reach the milestones you set in the next step.

HOME PLAY FOR DAYS 1 – 7

Over the next seven days, reflect and list your goals. Your goals must be meaningful and influenced by purpose.

YOUR NOTES HERE

PERSONAL GOALS

	GOAL	TIME FRAME	YOUR PURPOSE TO ACHIEVE THIS
1			
2			
3			
4			
5			
6			
7			
8			

PROFESSIONAL GOALS		
GOAL	TIME FRAME	YOUR PURPOSE TO ACHIEVE THIS
1		
2		
3		
4		
5		
6		
7		
8		

BUSINESS GOALS		
GOAL	TIME FRAME	YOUR PURPOSE TO ACHIEVE THIS
1		
2		
3		
4		
5		
6		
7		
8		

TIP TO THRIVE

"At least once a day allow yourself the freedom to think and dream."

ALBERT EINSTEIN
(C. 1879–1955)
THEORETICAL PHYSICIST

Albert Einstein aged 3
(Sourced from Wikipedia.)

Albert Einstein aged 25
(Sourced from Wikipedia.)

CASE STUDY

I worked with a lady in her mid-50s who came to me for help with business clarity.

She was a coach, well-educated and overall successful in her own right, but she was stuck on how to grow her business.

After two sessions of understanding of her background and business aspirations, in which we developed a 3D Diagnostic Review of her business, she started to gain great clarity.

I pointed her in the right direction to help her branding align with her service and target market, systemized delivery of her service to enhance client satisfaction, and placed the ball in her court, suggesting she add service policies and incorporate rules into introductory documents.

This far into her business transformation, with her newfound clarity, she grew in confidence and began receiving repeat business and referrals.

We continued to work towards meeting her objectives, focused on her end-game goals, and introduced her purpose-filled personal, professional and business goals.

As we continued to transform her business and her professional presence and brand, she said to me that she had seen many psychologists over the years to help her with long-standing issues, which were holding her back from both her childhood and 30 years ago. I was flattered and equally humbled to hear her say that the six sessions with me had essentially relieved her of the emotional baggage she was carrying.

Other clients have experienced similar break-throughs. I believe this is fundamentally due to this program's methodologies combined with the powerful session where I immerse myself in the client's scenario. Guiding them through solutions, I help them become the best they can be, and take their business to the next level.

"Unless you try to do something beyond what you have already mastered, you will never grow"

RONALD E. OSBORNE
(C. 1946–2014)
BRITISH-CANADIAN EXECUTIVE,
MAINLY IN MEDIA ORGANIZATIONS
AUTHOR

Every evening and morning, make time for yourself, and work through this ritual.

I do this exercise once a year, traditionally on Boxing Day, on a Sydney Beach.

For the greatest impact, read your goals daily.

Image by fuel for freedom on workpress.com

SYNOPSIS SNAPSHOT

- Set clear goals that align with purpose
- Read them each morning
- Share relevant goals with people you trust to keep you accountable. If you have a coach or mentor, share your goals with them to keep you accountable with measured support.

DAYS 1 – 7 OPTIONAL READ

THE POWER OF CLARITY

H.L. Hunt, a man who rose from a bankrupt cotton farmer in the 1930s to a multi-billionaire when he died in 1974, was once asked during a TV interview what advice he could give to others who wanted to be financially successful. He replied that only two things are required. First, you must decide exactly what it is you want to accomplish. Most people never do this in their entire lives. And secondly, he said, you must determine what price you'll have to pay to get it, and then resolve to pay that price.

CLEAR GOALS ARE ESSENTIAL

Clear goals and objectives are essential to the success of any business, and this is no less true of building your own career. If you don't take the time to get clear about exactly what it is you're trying to accomplish, then you're forever doomed to spend your life achieving the goals of those who do.

In the absence of a clear direction for your life, you will either meander aimlessly or you will build a career that you don't feel good about. You may make some money, and you may do some interesting work, but the end result will not resemble anything you ever made a conscious decision to build. Ultimately, you will be left with the sinking feeling that perhaps you took a wrong turn somewhere along the way. Do you ever look at your career and think to yourself, "How on earth did I get here?"

If setting goals is so critically important, why is it that so few people take the time to define exactly where they want to go? Part of the reason is a lack of knowledge about how to set clear goals. You can go through years of schooling and never receive any instruction on goal-setting. A failure to understand the immense importance of es- tablishing clear goals is also common. But those who truly know what they want often outperform everyone else by an enormous degree.

A frequent deterrent to goal-setting is the fear of making a mistake. Teddy Roosevelt once said, "In any moment of decision, the best thing you can do is the right thing, the next best thing is the wrong thing, and the worst thing you can do is nothing." Setting virtually any goal at all is better than drifting aimlessly with no clear direction. The best way I know to guarantee failure is to avoid making clear, committed decisions. Every day is already a mistake if you don't know where you're going. You're probably spending most of your time working to achieve other people's goals. The local fast-food restaurant, TV advertisers, and the stockholders of the businesses you patronize are all happy for that. If you don't decide what you really want, then you've decided to hand your future over to the whims of others, and that's always a mistake. By taking hold of the reins yourself and deciding where you'd like to go, you gain a tremendous sense of control that most people never experience in their entire lives.

Many people assume that because they have a direction they must therefore have goals, but this is not the case; it merely creates the illusion of progress. "Making more money" and "building a business" are not goals. A goal is a specific, clearly defined, measurable state. An example of the difference between a direction and a goal is the difference between the compass direction of northeast and the top of the Eiffel Tower in France. One is merely a direction; the other is a definite location.

DEFINE GOALS IN BINARY TERMS

One critical aspect of goals is that they must be defined in binary terms. At any point in time, if I were to ask you if you had achieved your goal yet, you must be able to give me a definitive "yes" or "no" answer; "maybe" is not an option. You cannot say with absolute certainty if you've fully completed the outcome of "making more money", but you can give me a definitive binary answer as to whether or not you are currently standing on top of the Eiffel Tower. An example of a clear business goal would be that your gross income for the month of April this year is $5,000 or more. That is something you can calculate precisely and, at the end of the month, you can give a definitive answer as to whether or not you have achieved your goal. This is the level of clarity you need in order to form a goal that your mind can lock onto and move towards rapidly.

BE DETAILED

Be as detailed as possible when setting goals. Give specific numbers, dates and times. Ensure that each of your goals is measurable. Either you achieved it, or you didn't. Define your goals as if you already know what's going to happen. It's been said that the best way to predict the future is to create it.

COMMIT GOALS TO WRITING

Goals must be in writing in the form of positive, present tense, and personal affirmations. A goal that is not committed to writing is just a fantasy. Set goals for what you want, not for what you don't want. Your subconscious mind can lock onto a clearly-defined goal only if the goal is defined in positive terms. If you put your focus on what you don't want instead of what you do, you're likely to attract exactly what it is you're trying to avoid. Phrase your goals as if they are already achieved. Instead of saying, "I will earn $100,000 this year," phrase it in the present tense: "I earn $100,000 this year." If you phrase your goals in future terms, you are sending a message to your subconscious mind to forever keep that outcome in the future, just beyond your grasp. Avoid wishy-washy words like "probably", "should", "could", "would", "might" or "may" when forming your goals. Such words foster doubt as to whether you can achieve what you are after. And finally, make your goals personal. You cannot set goals for other people, such as, "A publisher will publish my software by the end of the year." Phrase it like this instead: "I sign an Asia-Pacific retail publishing contract this year that earns me at least $100,000 by the end of the year."

OBJECTIFY SUBJECTIVE GOALS

What if you need to set subjective goals, such as improving your level of self-discipline? How do you measure such goals, or evaluate them in binary terms? To solve this problem, I use a rating scale from 1 to 10. For instance, if you want to improve your self-discipline, ask yourself on a scale of 1 to 10 how you rate your current level of self-discipline. Then set a goal to achieve a specific rating by a certain date. This scale allows you to measure your progress and know with a high degree of certainty whether or not you've reached your goal.

GOAL-SETTING IS AN ACTIVITY

Setting clear goals is not a passive act. It doesn't happen automatically. You must take direct, conscious action to make it so. Everything counts, and nothing is neutral. You are either moving toward your goals, or you're moving away from them. If you do nothing or if you act without clarity, then you are almost certainly a victim of "being out-goaled". In other words, you are spending your time working on other people's goals without even knowing it. You are happily working to enrich your landlord, other businesses, advertisers, stockholders, etc. Each day that you spend working without a sense of clarity about where you headed is a step backward for you. If you don't actively tend your garden, then weeds will grow. Weeds don't need to be watered or fertilized. They grow by them- selves in the absence of an attentive gardener. Similarly, in the absence of conscious and directed action on your part, your work and your life will automatically become full of weeds. You don't need to do anything at all to make this happen. And when you finally get around to taking a serious look at where you are and where you want to go, the first thing you will have to do is pull out all those weeds.

Reading this advice will do absolutely nothing for you unless you turn it into some form of physical action. Even the best thinking, unfortunately, yields you zero results. In reality, you won't be paid a penny for your thoughts. You can have the most creative idea in the world, but ideas themselves are utterly worthless. You only get results from the physical actions you take, never for the ideas you have. For any tangible results, you must act on an idea. You must communicate it, build it, implement it, and make it real.

CLARITY IS A CHOICE

If you have run your career in an unfocused manner, waking up each morning and seeing what happens, then it is crucial that you take the time to decide and write down exactly where it is you want to go. How much longer will you continue to climb the ladder of success, only to realize too late that it was leaning against the wrong building? Pick a point in the future, whether it's six months from now or five years from now, and spend a few hours writing out a clear description of where you want to be at that time. I know many people who aren't sure where they want to go, so they avoid committing anything to writing in order to "keep their options open". What would happen if you pursued that attitude to its logical conclusion? If you always kept your options open without making any firm commitments, then you'd never get promoted, start your own business, get married, have a family, move to that new home, or achieve any number of life's milestones—except to the degree that someone else made that decision for you.

I had a friend like this who still hasn't decided what he wants to do with his life. He passes control of his life to others, without even realizing it, simply because he's unwilling to take the time to define a vision for his own life out of fear of making the wrong choice. His life is ruled by those who push their goals onto him, which he accepts by default. Ask yourself if you are in the same boat. If a friend became committed to getting you to change something in your life at random—your career, your living situation, your relationship—could they do it by simply remaining certain and committed that it was the right thing for you? Could a business associate come along and radically alter your plans for the week without you ever deciding consciously that such a change is consistent with your goals? We all suffer from problems like these, but only to the degree that we fail to set clear goals for ourselves. There is a big difference between recognizing and acting on a true opportunity and being knocked off course without making a conscious decision to shift gears.

Waiting for something to inspire you and hoping that the perfect outcome will just fall into your lap is nothing but a fantasy. Clear decision-making doesn't happen passively; you must physically devote the time to make it happen. If you don't have clear goals because you don't know what you want, then sit down and actively decide what you want. That sense of knowing what you want isn't going to come to you in the form of divine inspiration. Clarity is a choice, not an accident or a gift. Clarity doesn't come to you—you must go to it. Not setting goals is the same as deciding to be a slave to the goals of others.

CLEAR GOALS SHARPEN PRESENT MOMENT DECISIONS

Your reality will not match your vision precisely. That's not the point. The point is that your vision allows you to make clear decisions daily that keep you moving in the direction of your goals. When a commercial airliner flies from one city to another, it is off-course over 90% of the time, but it keeps measuring its progress and adjusting its heading again and again. Goal-setting works the same way. Maintain a clear list of goals, not because that's actually where you will end up, but because it will give you tremendous certainty in deciding what you need to do today. When someone contacts you with an "opportunity" out of the blue, you'll know whether it is a real opportunity or a waste of time. The long-term view sharpens the short-term view.

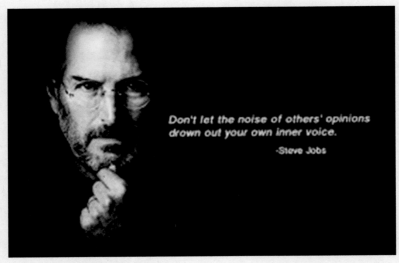

Image sourced from Goalcast.

As you begin moving toward your goals, you will gain knowledge along the way, and you must adapt your plans as you go. You may also change your vision if you get partway there and decide it's not quite what you want. Ill-formed goals are still far superior to no goals at all.

Someone once told me that I should end each day by crossing it off my calendar and saying out loud, "There goes another day of my life, never to return again." Try this for yourself, and notice how much it sharpens your focus. When you end a day with the feeling that you would have lived it the same if you had the chance to repeat it, you gain a sense of gratitude that helps you focus on what is important to you. When you end the day with a feeling of regret or loss, you gain awareness to try a different approach the next day.

You'll see a measurable difference in your life from the first day you establish clear, committed goals, even if your first few attempts are not perfect. You will be able to make decisions more rapidly because you will see how they either move you towards or away from your goals. On the eve of his death, Walt Disney had a reporter crawl into bed with him, so he could share his vision for Disney World, six years before its completion. When Disney World finally opened, another reporter commented to Walt's brother, Roy, "It's too bad Walt did not live to see this." Roy replied, "Walt saw it first. That's why we are seeing it now." Clear goals allow you to achieve the first half of H.L. Hunt's success formula. By deciding exactly what you want to accomplish, committing it to writing, and reviewing it on a daily basis, you bring your goals into reality with the power of your focus.

EXTRA HOME PLAY AT
THE ACADEMY OF BUSINESS

Log onto Academy of Business/Discovery to access the following templates to aid further success:

- SMART Goals
- Include milestone and the 3-month goals template
- Include the business plan template

CHAPTER TWO
DESIGN AND ALIGN

DAYS 8 – 14

MY STORY

Over 22 years ago, I began my business journey as a young entrepreneur. I was 17 years old when I started in business, so I can completely relate to what it is like to have a dream and start out as a green business owner. With literally no more than this dream, but with passion, drive and determination to back myself, I took ownership of the business I was working in. I saw it as an opportunity to fulfill my ambition of owning and running my first business and growing the business to new levels.

This business experience was my "real-life MBA". With each phase of business obstacles and opportunities, I used common sense to identify the business's needs and gaps, finding solutions to take the business to the next level.

Over two decades on, I have enjoyed the privilege of gaining experience through starting up, buying, developing, re-branding then merging and selling more than ten self-owned businesses in a range of industries. All came to fruition by taking calculated risks and "having a go".

An injury in 2008 turned my world upside down. Until then, I controled my world by achieving everything I set out to accomplish in my business with minimal setbacks. This injury, however, pushed me into a new dimension. For the first time in my life, I felt that I didn't have full control. This unexpected injury pushed me out of my comfort zone and forced me to instantly change my career path. I didn't have a Plan B, nor the recognized skills to jump straight into something else and earn well.

Until this time, I had lived at a fast, successful pace and life ran according to "my" plan. Suddenly, I faced a situation that challenged my fast-flowing, high-flying life. I was used to planning, preparing and achieving with full control of the throttle and reins, so I found myself in an extremely uncomfortable and foreign space.

At the time, my husband said to me, "You have been working since you were 13 years old. Take three months out to reflect, update your skills if you like, and look into what is the best next step for you in business."

So I did.

This was the turning point in my business path. The doom and gloom I felt after the injury placed me on a three-month, life-changing sabbatical. I embarked on a brand new journey, exploring ground I never thought I would.

I moved forward by firstly listing what I didn't want to do. I then wrote down the type of business I wanted to pursue. This process of elimination brought great clarity.

When I combined my experience and skills—developed over years of managing various businesses at all phases of the business life cycle—with the new emotions that surfaced while reflecting and looking for answers, I started to see what the next chapter should look like.

This sabbatical, in hindsight, became the highlight in my making.

It transformed the way that I did business and how I helped others achieve their business and personal goals.

Since starting as a consultant, I have been blessed with amazing opportunities to help businesses reach their potential through transformative projects, after aligning my client's personal and professional goals.

Interestingly, clients and stakeholders alike have brought to my attention my ability to walk into a business and quickly identify its strengths, weaknesses and required improvements, and communicate clearly how to fix them. Clients tell me that I communicate and work effectively with people from different levels in a business—from the administration staff to technicians to middle management and up to the CEO and Chairman of the board.

My skills and experience allow me to identify the root of issues quickly and diligently, implementing result-oriented solutions that turn around a business in the quickest timeframe.

"A goal without a plan is just a wish"

ANONYMOUS

DESIGN AND ALIGN TEACHINGS

The next step is creating your Action Plan. This will help you bring your goals to life.

Before we start this next step, we need to reflect on the past seven days. As you were internalizing, reflecting and dreaming of what you wanted your future to look like, did you at any stage get that odd feeling inside that you were visualizing your future? Were you able to remove all the blocks?

Remember, feelings act as a gauge, alerting us if we are on the right track or if we are to proceed with caution. Our subconscious connects with our feelings to bring us these messages. As we proceed, it is vital that we remain in-tune with ourselves, picking up subliminal messages sent by our feelings— known as intuition. If you are motivated, you must then articulate your intuition to help break through blocks and obstacles, which form the core that stops you from successfully achieving or proceeding to the next level to become the person you want to be and having the business and lifestyle you want.

Constructive "time out" for yourself is vital—it is your time to connect with your intuition and feelings, reflect on your goals and schedule, and be creative. Time out allows you to identify potential blocks that may appear and articulate your intuition for growth and self-development.

As life is so busy, time out for yourself is imperative, so you can stay in tune and pick up on these messages and feelings, and go through the process of releasing them to be free and have clarity and confidence to continue on a positive path towards your dreams.

Throughout my time working with smart and successful leaders, I have identified a common trend of suffering—a suffering recently labeled as the "Imposter's Syndrome".

Do you ever feel that you are not good enough to live the life you envisaged or to have your current career? Do you feel unworthy to grow your business to meet your goals?

You may have heard about this before, and you may also be suffering from Imposter Syndrome.

Many accomplished, successful, famous and well-known people suffer from this. You would never know, as they are in high positions and they look confident from the outside, but feel different on the inside.

Could this be you?

You may appear confident and capable, but a voice on the inside is saying, "I don't feel I should be here...I don't belong here."

This embedded belief affects many successful people, possibly like you, and it affects their ability to reach their personal best in all areas of life.

You must bring this belief to the surface, become friends with that deep inner voice, and nurture the insecurity. If the insecurity is around public speaking, keep doing more and more of it until you feel like you belong there. Whatever the insecurity relates to, acknowledge it and put your hand up, volunteering to repeat this task until you feel you own it with inner confidence. Understand how you process the task from the initial thought, then mindfully work through each stage of the process through to accomplishment.

I remember when I was extremely nervous about public speaking, or before attending an event where I had to introduce myself to people I had never met.

Although I knew that no one could tell how I was feeling inside and how nervous I was, rationalizing it in that way did not make me feel better and I could not overcome my nerves. I have a naturally confident presence, so people don't recognize that I am also shy and prefer to converse with a small group or one on one.

Then, one evening as I drove alone to a large event, I had a thought, which I took ownership of. I recall confidently telling myself, "I am nervous to speak in front of new people…I am shy." You will not believe what happened next.

The fear went away.

I realized that if you can acknowledge, embrace and accept who you are, you will blossom with confidence.

I attended that business event and met new people without fear and was not nervous.

Image sourced from Twitter.com

HOME PLAY FOR DAYS 8 – 14

TWELVE MONTH ACTION PLAN		
What do you need to do achieve your goal? Do you need to make changes in your schedule to achieve your goal?	Completed	
	Yes	No
Personal Goals		
Professional Goals		
Business Goals		

Over the next seven days, complete this Action Plan. Think about your goals and visualize what your life is about to look like.

 TIP TO THRIVE

"You will become what You Believe. You will achieve what You Visualize."

Adriana Cecere

CASE STUDY

The Professor's Ear Nose Throat Clinics

Time:
11 months.

The Scope:
Business Development.

Issues:
The business operation needed leadership. Like most outstanding and busy professionals, the Professor didn't have all the skills, desire or time to work on business development, manage staff, implement new systems, and dive into the daily operation to optimize departments. In this instance, the Professor was already generating $10,000 - $50,000 + revenue each day and making good profits, but was lacking the skill and time to optimize the business operation to run better.

Results Achieved:

Each department was reviewed, client spending was analyzed, and clear benchmarks were set on what an ideal client or hospital department should look like. Stakeholder relationships were built to benefit the practice, and the staff's wellbeing was nurtured. These measures improved a dysfunctional workplace where the team was unhappy, despite satisfied clients and the business generating a massive profit. Adriana introduced inductions, 2-way performance reviews, staff contracts, and birthday and Christmas team celebrations to build a better workplace environment.

Out of Scope Results:

Adriana sourced and project managed new CRM and operational software system change from PC to Mac across the three clinics. She also systemized the clinics, rolled out an operational manual, and introduced HR management and a paperless office.

How We Did It:
With professional tact, focusing on delivering high-level strategies, good use of people management skills, and business management and development strategies.

Why Adriana:
Experience in developing businesses and good people skills.

SYNOPSIS SNAPSHOT

- To achieve sustainable success, you must identify both your personal and professional goals
- These goals must be aligned—if they aren't, you are at risk of suffering internal conflict, which will impact your long term success
- Develop and hone your success mindset
- You have identified core issues and solutions to take your business to its next level
- You have designed and formulated a strategic implementation plan to apply solutions to correct the business
- Revise your Action Plan daily

"*Success is the sum of small efforts, repeated day in and day out*"

ROBERT COLLIER
(c. 1885–1950)
AUTHOR
FOUNDER OF COLLIER MOTORS

DAYS 8 – 14 OPTIONAL READING

STRATEGIC PLANNING

Implementing your Strategic Plan is fundamental to achieving your business goals.

As a consultant, I work alongside your employees and management, will provide recommendations useful in aligning business expectations with the team's performance.

At this stage, all aspects of company policies, customer satisfaction, brand awareness, and marketing will be analyzed with the aim of ensuring the correct position of the organization in the market. This mentoring will be useful at the end of the implementation stage, before moving into the optimization stage, to establish synergy within the organization.

Now that you have clear goals and milestones, and a strategic plan, it is time to integrate these—aligning them with your business operation.

Layer your learnings. At first, the process was like peeling an onion as we stripped off layer upon layer of what was not useful.

Next, we rebuilt your foundation with a new direction, including a new mindset, establishing clear goals that provided you with clarity and greater confidence.

EXTRA HOME PLAY AT
THE ACADEMY OF BUSINESS

Log onto Academy of Business/Design and Align to access the following templates to aid further Success:

- Business Review Template

Once complete, this template enables you to review your business performance in great detail. There is a summary below.

REVIEW CHECKLIST SUMMARY

Consider the following areas:

- Sales
- Operation
- Finances
- Administration
- Marketing
- Branding

Look deeper—what is working and what needs improving in the following areas?

- Customer Satisfaction
- Employee and Stakeholder Satisfaction
- Productivity
- Cash Flow
- Gross Margin
- Do you have a strong Value Proposition?

"Success is not final;
failure is not fatal:
It is the courage
to continue that
counts"

Sir Winston S. Churchill
(c. 1874–1965)
British statesman, army officer and writer
United Kingdom Prime Minister

CHAPTER THREE
TRANSFORMATION
DAYS 15 – 21

MY STORY—IN THE BEGINNING

Reflecting back on what I wanted to do with my life after completing school…

I vividly remember being about 12 years of age. I was with my younger brother, Rob, at the old farmhouse where I was born and raised. We were both standing by our pushbikes under the kitchen window near the massive bay leaf tree, goofing around and chatting. I remember asking Rob, "What do you want to do when you finish school?" I then told him I wanted to have a business by the time I was 18 years old.

My father would often ask us these types of questions, in his broken English-Italian, around what we wanted to do when we grew up. So this was a typical conversation in our family. In that conversation with Rob, I remember counting with my fingers how many years it would be before I could leave school and get into the real world. I wanted to start full-time work before ultimately embarking on my business journey.

From that moment and the conversation with Rob, until I started in business, I had that thought planted firmly in my mind. I often thought about that dream.

At the time, I was already working a part-time job in our neighbor's nursery, after school and on weekends. I continued working until I finished school in Grade 10, to start an apprenticeship. I recall how older family members were not keen for me to drop out of school. They all had degrees and were employed straight after University. It makes sense that they were genuinely concerned I was making the wrong choice. Regardless, I continued to follow my dreams and left school to take on the apprenticeship. I began my first business just two years later.

The initial part of my business journey taught me the benefits of having goals and dreaming about the direction you want to take in life. Owning a business was important to me.

When I was 17 years old, nearly three years into my apprenticeship, I was in a conversation about a business sale—it was music to my ears. I wanted to own a business by 18 years of age, and got excited by potential opportunities to take action.

By the age of 17 years and nine months, I had become a business owner. I didn't realize it at the time, but now, many years later, I am aware of the powerful benefit of visualizing and having dreams.

"If you want something you've never had you must be willing to do something you've never done"

ANONYMOUS

TRANSFORMATION TEACHINGS

You are now in a position where you have taken a Deep Dive to identify your personal, professional and business goals. It has been 14 days since you adopted the morning and evening ritual of visualizing the great picture in mind and owned the path and outcomes of your business and lifestyle.

Over the past seven days, you have mapped out what you must do and change to start taking the first steps on your new path, if you have not already started.

In the next seven days, you will bring it all together. To ensure a successful transformation, you must be held accountable. You will need to document and track your progress. It is wise to tell people around you who will encourage you to take this next step. Tell them that you are undertaking this 28-day transformation journey, so that they can support you. It could be your personal assistant, operations manager, life partner, children, parent or friend. If you have a mentor or coach, you must tell them for they will be underpinning your success. If you don't yet have a coach, now might be the right time to get one. If it's not the right time for you for whatever reason, don't worry, I have drafted the worksheet below, so you can track your performance to change and hold yourself accountable.

Now is the time to start walking the talk and taking action.

Smart leaders I have worked with have a way of getting into a success mindset that resonates with them. They have a special trigger, like pressing their thumb and middle finger together, which brings them into an instant mindset shift that connects them to a vision with confidence. They use during challenging situations, or before important meetings or interviews. If you don't have your own trigger, Amy Caddy has coined one called the "Power Pose".

To access this video, log onto the Academy of Business portal.

Below you will find the worksheet to help you become accountable over the next seven days as you step into your new path.

Before we move onto home play, here are some additional points to help you prepare.

Once complete, each morning for the next seven days as you awake and step out of bed, say THANK YOU.

Before you do anything else, or if you have children to attend to as soon as you can before you get into the thick of things, go to a quiet space, and set off your trigger, or power pose.

Read your goals and visualize what your life will look like, smell like and feel like in ten years. Smile and take three deep breaths of confidence and proud ownership of accomplishment.

Open your eyes, and get to your worksheet. Allow this to be your guide, and complete it daily.

At the end of each day, reflect on your achievements and what can be improved.

Don't expect everything to fall into place after day one. Remember, if you are making significant changes, for anything great to be achieved, it will take time to do well.

Each day, continue celebrating your achievements and identifying improvements. If you have a coach, reach out to them for support; they will support you. Work through things with others related to your goals, such as your personal assistant, life partner, business partner, board or operations manager. Bringing in all of these support people on areas that relate to them will bring more power for you to achieve your goals. If they are not supportive, reflect on why. If they are negative towards the changes, you must consider if they are the right person to fill that support role in your life and business. Invite them on the 28-day journey with you—they may need help unblocking their own negative beliefs from the past. If they are open to this, it will be a grand scenario.

"Wake up with determination. Go to bed with satisfaction!"

Anonymous

HOME PLAY FOR DAYS 15 – 21

Over the next seven days, build Accountability into your Action Plan.

MEASURED ACCOUNTABILITY					
Goal	Action	Changes to schedule	New skills	Completed Yes	No

TIP TO THRIVE

"Whatever the mind can conceive and believe, the mind can achieve."

Napoleon Hill
(c. 1883–1970)
Author of 10 best-sellers,
including *Think and Grow Rich*

Adriana Cecere, accolade acceptance speech in London, on 7th December 2017. Recognition as a Global Leader for Excellence in Innovation.

CASE STUDY

I had a client that was a globally-recognized brand. Its business growth and brand recognition were driven by the board, yet serviced by a CEO and team who operated reactively; they were short of skills to develop the business operation to meet increasing market demand and the needs of their clients, members, and stakeholders.

The President and Vice President of the board called me in to conduct a three-week business review.

On day 1, it was clear that the business operations lacked direction as the CEO was under-skilled. The team was working exceptionally and unnecessarily hard due to lack of guidance, processes and systems, and the company's operations were dysfunctionally unaligned with the vision of the board members.

In my first week, the CEO was asked to resign. As a result, most of the team resigned too. In the interim, I was asked to step in and rescue the business.

With diligence and skill, in six months I had introduced into the business most of what was needed in a startup, including re-cruiting new team members and satisfying both stakeholders' and members' needs until a long-term CEO was appointed. This was a detailed yet rewarding project.

SYNOPSIS SNAPSHOT

- Visualize your future as a reality daily
- Identify shifts and changes you need to make to begin aligning actions to achieve your goals
- Start implementing changes into your life on day one

"Hustle & heart will set up apart"

Anonymous

DAYS 15 – 21 OPTIONAL READING

FIVE STEPS TO A
SUCCESSFUL TRANSFORMATION

It has been said that the only constant in business is change. Meanwhile, numerous studies have shown that up to 70% of change efforts fail. Luckily for managers, this does not have to be the case. With proper planning, thoughtful management, and appropriate timelines, even the largest of complex change initiatives will be successful. Change initiatives can vary widely in scope and complexity. Large-scale projects are typically at the enterprise or business unit level, while small-scale projects could be at the program or process level. Business transformation typically refers to medium and large scale projects that impact strategies, management systems, or multiple business processes. Large-scale transformations may result from the acquisition of a new company, market disruption, business model innovation, restructuring for revenue growth, or performance improvement and operational change.

Once the need for change is recognized, either due to an event similar to those above or through identifying a specific performance gap, the transformative journey can begin. The five-step process below, combines multiple operational and change management methodologies into one easily applied framework. It can serve as a guide for organizations undertaking business transformation on any scale.

STEP ONE:
COMPLETE A CURRENT STATE ASSESSMENT

To effectively transform a business, you must first understand the current state of its operations. Current State Assessment includes developing an understanding of the current strategy, measuring baselines for key performance metrics, mapping various business processes, outlining the staff's existing skill sets, and documenting the capabilities of technology and information systems. Once understood, the business's current state is best communicated through two specific tools: the SIPOC (Supplier → Input → Process → Output → Customer) diagram, and the organizational alignment matrix. The operational aspects of business can be mapped using the SIPOC, while the organizational alignment matrix can holistically document the business landscape (Strategy, Management System, Processes, Technology, People and Organization).

STEP TWO:
ESTABLISH AN ORGANIZATIONAL STRATEGY

The organizational strategy establishes initial parameters governing the business's transformation. Assuming the entity being transformed is not an entire company, the strategy that applies most directly to the transformation is that of the affected business unit itself. It is important to note, however, that this micro-level strategy should be supportive of the company's macro-level strategic direction.

A simple approach to strategy for business transformation typically contains four components:

- a Mission Statement
- a Vision Statement
- Core Values (typically those of the larger entity), and
- Guiding Principles (for the transformation initiative itself)

An important distinction must be made between Mission and Vision statements: while the Mission Statement defines the organization's purpose, the Vision Statement outlines its future aspirations, or what it hopes to be "post-transformation".

STEP THREE:
DEVELOP AN ORGANIZATIONAL CHANGE MANAGEMENT PLAN

The logical step after conducting the Current State Assessment and developing the organizational strategy may seem to be designing the future state. Proceeding to that step immediately, however, would place the success of transformation in doubt. Given that a business transformation is by nature a transformational change for the whole organization, it is critical to consider and plan for its impact on all aspects of the business and its employees. Organizational Change Management (OCM) is the "soft" side of business transformation. While numerous technical considerations help to define and implement the future state vision, the focus of OCM is to make employees aware of, and engaged in, the change effort. Executed properly, OCM can remove obstructions that prevent change from occurring, accelerate the transformation, and positively impact post-transformation sustainment. Three common components of OCM are stakeholder analyses, communication plans, and training plans. The communication component of OCM is critical to successful business transformation. If employees and stakeholders do not understand the purpose and vision for the change initiative, they may become resistant, stopping progress in its tracks. Effective communication plans often overcome these challenges by communicating the vision for change repeatedly and through all available channels.

STEP FOUR:
DESIGN THE FUTURE STATE AND DEVELOP AN IMPLEMENTATION PLAN

Once the need for Organizational Change Management has been accepted, business transformation can proceed to designing the Future State and developing an Implementation Plan. Once complete by the organization, this step will have defined the way forward and developed a plan for making the business vision a reality. Using the organizational strategy as a starting point, business leaders must outline technical aspects of proposed changes. Re-visit the Organizational Alignment model from Step One to test the completeness and alignment of the future design. Is the organizational strategy supported by adequate measurement and management systems? Do the processes and technology solutions achieve the desired results relative to the strategy? Are the organization's resources (employees or equipment) aligned to the new production system? If the answer to each of these questions is "yes" then management can proceed to develop an implementation plan that, in concert with the Organizational Change Management Plan, can be enacted to turn the aspirational vision into reality.

STEP FIVE: IMPLEMENT CHANGES AND SUSTAIN IMPROVEMENTS

Although implementation and sustainment are the final components of business transformation, plenty of risks to success remain. Rushing implementation can place extreme pressure on existing operations and staff, resulting in the re-emergence of employees' resistance to change. Business leaders must be careful to ensure that the change initiative doesn't fall victim to "the way we've always done it".

The most direct method to ensuring a proper pace of implementation is to follow these steps: apply the Plan, Do, Check, Act (PDCA). The PDCA model is commonly used in lean management. It dictates that required changes are made one at a time and in proper sequence. This meticulous approach allows each change to be properly implemented, measured, and adjusted as needed before moving on to the next item on the implementation plan.

Implementing multiple changes to a system at once makes it difficult to ensure that each change is having a positive effect.

Another benefit of the PDCA model is that it can help drive a post-transformation, continuous improvement program—a critical component to ongoing sustainment.

Following these five steps in sequence, and with realistic timelines, will be a leap in the right direction for any business transformation initiative.

TIP TO THRIVE

"True leadership is about making other people better as a result of your presence— and making sure your impact endures in your absence.

HARVARD BUSINESS SCHOOL;

LEADERSHIP DEFINITION

"*People don't care about your business. They care about their problems. Be the solution that they are looking for*"

ANONYMOUS

THE FIVE PRINCIPLES OF PERSONAL TRANSFORMATION

ONE.
APPRECIATE YOUR SUCCESS.

This first principle is a challenge. We are quick to criticize and slow to praise—especially when it comes to our relationship with ourselves.

It's not surprising. Our world focuses on bad news. Newspapers, magazines, television and the Internet—all generate a negative environment. So we find it all too easy to focus on what's wrong. When we achieve something, often we discount it because, after all, *I* did it—how great can it be?

Failure to live this first principle drains our confidence and keeps us stuck, instead of on the path to where we want to be.

Start by appreciating your successes and the success of others.

By staying in touch with your accomplishments, you build true, authentic confidence to move on to make new things happen.

Appreciating your success enables you to take responsibility for your greatness so that your life isn't about becoming good enough, but about finding ways to use your gifts to make a difference.

It is not wrong to praise and appreciate yourself. You will not become arrogant. You will not become more egocentric. Rather, you will inspire yourself, and perhaps others, to do bigger things.

TWO.
LEARN YOUR LESSONS.

Review your past year to discover what worked and what didn't—find the lessons you need to learn. You are your own best teacher and the best source of your own wisdom. We never really need advice, and we hate receiving it because we're being told what we know already!

It's essential to learn from your success and your failures. First, catch yourself doing things right and incorporate that success into your future. Next, review your mistakes and disappointments to discover the advice you need to follow to do better next time.

Once you capture your lessons, boil them down to memorable pieces of advice to remember in the next week, month or year. Limit yourself to the three most important lessons; there is only so much we can truly learn at one time. Example lessons are:

- Remember what matters
- Take care of myself
- Confront issues early
- Remain positive

I have been making a personal Best Year Yet plan for over 2 decades, and this step of learning my lessons has been invaluable. There is always something more to learn. But the joy is that I rarely have to learn the same lessons over and over again—I get to tackle new ones!

THREE.
SHIFT YOUR LIMITING BELIEFS.

Until we wake up to the negative beliefs we have about our chances for success, we live in a small box that limits what is possible.

Here is what happens: when we aren't getting the results we want, we change what we're doing. But, if your results don't change, it is because you have a strong limiting belief that is controlling your actions.

Both the right attitude and the right action are necessary to achieve the right results. Both are necessary to become a master at producing results. This principle is the heart of the matter. Your actions are guided by what you assume to be true: your attitude. Examples of negative self-talk include:

- "I don't know enough to..."
- "He/she's a lot better than I am at..."
- "I'm too old to..."
- "I can't do that because I don't have..."
- "I haven't got time to..."

Find what you think is true about you and cannot be changed, no matter what you do. That's the limiting belief to shift. Start the attack by accepting that this belief is your invention. As long as you live as if this statement is true and nothing you do can change it, you have no chance of success.

To achieve a personal transformation, develop a new belief that clearly states the reality you want to create. Make sure the statement is positive, in the present tense, and is as powerful and exciting as you can make it.

- People are lucky to have me working for them
- I have what it takes to make a lot more money
- I handle anything that comes my way

Keep repeating your new paradigm until you realize that this is the truth and that your old limiting belief was a lie and does not belong to you.

"Great things in business are never done by one person. They're done by a team of people"

STEVE JOBS
(C. 1955–2011)
CO-FOUNDER OF APPLE COMPUTERS

FOUR.
LIVE YOUR VALUES.

It is easy to criticize others because of the noticeable gap between their behavior and the values they espouse. But doing so is not a good use of our time, to say the least.

What makes sense is examining our own lives in light of what we believe, our values. When we don't live by them, we suffer. One of my early teachers taught that our lack of integrity is the source of all our suffering.

For example, if one of your values is honesty, yet you find yourself pushing your hidden agenda instead of taking care of the person in front of you, you suffer inside, right? Learn to shift immediately when you become aware that what you do does not align with your personal values.

FIVE.
SET AND TRACK YOUR TOP 10 GOALS.

Once you start living the first four principles, you will become more in touch with what matters to you. You are more aware of what you can do; you have guidelines to learn your lessons and a new paradigm to sustain your transformation; and you are awake to your personal values.

Now it's time to get specific about your priorities for the next year. You are ready to put your personal transformation into action—to make a living, breathing and demonstrable difference in your world and beyond.

Write no more than 10 goals that will make the next year your best year yet, in both your personal and professional life. Set, track, and score monthly goals that are the steps toward your yearlong goals.

Soon you will feel more like the master of your own destiny than you have in many years—and you will enjoy what it feels like to do what matters to you.

EXTRA HOME PLAY AT
THE ACADEMY OF BUSINESS

Log onto Academy of Business/Transformation to access the following templates to aid further success:

- Business Plan
- Business Operation Report. The ultimate performance report providing a snapshot of how your business is tracking in real time while you are on the run

 TIP TO THRIVE

*"Your level of success is a
direct outcome of your effort."*

ADRIANA CECERE

CHAPTER FOUR
OPTIMIZATION
DAYS 22 – 28

MY STORY— STRIVING FOR EXCELLENCE

After my injury in 2008, I unpacked what my future business could look like by firstly identifying what I didn't want to do and could not do due to the injury in my future career and business. Through this sabbatical and traumatic reflection period, it became clear that I had the experience and skills to identify business performance and how to fix it.

After seeing what I had achieved, business leaders started approaching me to help them rescue, align, and grow their businesses. I could feel this was my next step and business; I was passionate and enjoyed this work.

I realized quickly that I needed to hone skills and articulate my intuition into frameworks, so I could offer my clients the best service. I engaged a coach to help me clarify and articulate my intuition into programs and blueprints.

This proved a powerful move as, by this stage, I was already busy with clients and needed guidance to hasten development of my toolkit.

To my pleasant surprise, my business catapulted as a result. I still engage coaches to help me remain at the top of my game in innovation and clarity, so I can offer my clients the best possible service.

Striving for excellence and optimizing my service and skills by speaking to a coach and learning from each client review is a powerful formula to stay true to myself and offer the best to my clients.

OPTIMIZATION TEACHINGS

Congratulations, you are commencing Week Four. It takes 21 days to break a habit, and you are now on to Day 22. Your focus over the next seven days and beyond is to continue with this process and see what you can do to improve and achieve your goals with ease.

"As you hustle along your journey to success, never forget how far you have already travelled"

AJ KULATUNGA
AUTHOR
ENTREPRENEUR

HOME PLAY FOR DAYS 22 – 28

Over the next seven days, introduce the following Good Habits into your existing daily routine:

1: ALWAYS ADD VALUE.

Value makes the world go round. Everyone wants to get value out of an exchange. The most successful entrepreneurs in the world know that if you're going to make lots of money, then you need to always be adding value. Always seek to add more value to whatever services, information or products you are selling.

2: WAKE UP EARLY.

The early morning hours are replete with quiet solitude. That's when you can refine your thoughts and implement your plans before all the distractions of the day begin. If you are constantly dealing with interruptions throughout the day, find your happy place in the morning. Wake up early so you can plan whatever will advance you toward your goals.

3: EXERCISE

Making money isn't just about implementing good career or business habits. You need to be fit emotionally and physically to fire on all pistons. Exercise in the morning, even if briefly. Exercising gets the blood flowing and oxygenates the cells, helping you think clearly and be laser-focused. This habit is common to many of the world's richest entrepreneurs.

4: SET DAILY GOALS.

You have your long-term goals in place but, if you're looking to make serious money quickly, you must set mini-goals every single day. These are milestones on your way to your biggest and most outlandish goals. Do this when you wake up, first thing in the morning, so that you stay on track and on target. Decide what will move you closer to those financial goals by the end of the day, then go out there and do it.

5: MANAGE YOUR TIME EFFECTIVELY.

Everyone in this world has the same amount of time. The 24 hours of each day is life's greatest equalizer. It doesn't matter what we do, where we're from, or how much money we have, we all have the same amount of time.

Effective time management is a must for those looking to get ahead. Whether your goal is to earn a lot of money over time or you just need to earn a little bit of extra cash quickly, properly managing your finite time is what makes it possible to succeed.

6: NETWORK.

Networking is one of the most important habits to have in life. As the saying goes, "your network is your net worth", and "if you lie down with dogs, you'll get up with fleas".

Reach out to others and find out what you can do to add value to their world. Don't ask for anything in return, especially not right away. Just insert yourself into the mix Eventually, opportunities will find you.

7: INNERCISE.

John Assaraf, who built up a billion-dollar real estate business and is featured in the movie *The Secret*, preaches the importance of "innercising" in his NeuroGym system. Innercising is mental exercise to re-program subliminal conditioning deeply embedded in our subconscious. The goal is to frame the mind with a positive financial outlook, which attracts money and opportunities to our lives, rather than pushing them away.

8: EAT A HEALTHY DIET.

Will eating healthier help you attract more wealth or make more money in the interim? You can bet it will. A sound body means a sound mind. To have the precision thinking and focus of a highly trained athlete, you need to eat healthily. Our bodies spend a large amount of their energy processing food. Unhealthy eating leaves us with less energy for achieving our goals, whatever they are.

9: SAVE AND INVEST.

Obviously, saving and investing is fundamental to building wealth. It won't happen as fast as you'd like, but the larger component at play is having moment-of-the-opportunity cash to invest when something requires your attention immediately. When you have capital and are no longer living paycheck-to-paycheck, you are ready to earn more money when the opportunity presents.

10: PRACTICE MINDFULNESS.

If you play a cut-throat game and walk all over people, few opportunities will come your way. Being mindful and respectful of others attracts opportunities that you can eventually convert into cash. Be mindful about how you act and what you say, so it doesn't come back to bite you in the butt.

11: WORK WITH A MENTOR.

Mentors are great for helping you earn extra income, whether small or large. A mentor who has achieved outlandish goals in your industry will offer guidance to help you get where you are looking to go. Find a mentor and work with them daily. Ask for their help and guidance as you navigate the choppy waters toward success.

12: CONTRIBUTE TO OTHERS.

Contribution is born from an abundant mindset. When you are sated and have enough for yourself, look to contribute. You can trick your mind into an abundant mindset by simply contributing your time to others. You don't have to give money. Only time. It's a subconscious mind trick that moves you away from scarcity to attract more money and opportunities into your life.

13: RISE ABOVE ALL AND SHIFT YOUR MINDSET TO ONE OF AN IDEALIST.

High-achievers bring a positive attitude to everything they do. They believe in themselves and in their ideas, and they believe that obstacles can be overcome. Failure is accepted as a natural part of business and as an opportunity to learn and improve.

Shift your model from doing it on your own. If you are not already doing so, start relying more on others. Far from being the independent mavericks that we see in the movies, successful people and high-achievers know that they can't do it alone. They surround themselves with smart, reliable and honest people and value their skills and feedback.

TIP TO THRIVE

*"If you put others first selflessly,
they will lift you up."*

ADRIANA CECERE

CASE STUDY

While my husband and I were moving house and potentially just hours away from me giving birth, I took a phone call. It was the CEO of an iconic global sporting organization. He sounded distressed and wanted to meet with me as soon as possible.

Among the boxes and furniture, which had just been delivered by Kent removals, I went looking for my 'meeting' maternity dress. I found it hanging and still a little wet as it had just been washed. I blow-dried it a little then put on the slightly damp dress, pulled my hair back to look presentable, and left my husband to unpack more boxes, explaining, "I'll be back in a couple of hours." I drove to meet with the President and Vice President of the board. This business was in a pickle and they needed urgent help.

The night before giving birth, the President called me again; he needed further advice.

The next morning, I called him back offering advice before heading to the hospital to have our baby. During the call, he asked me if I could submit a proposal to help the business. I explained that I would work on it over the next few days in hospital, and that he would have it by Friday.

The day after having our baby, I started drafting the proposal. Separately, I started noting various ways I could help this business. I emailed the President the proposal on the Friday, as promised. He appreciated my work and effort.

Three weeks later, I began attending their office a few days a week on a highly complex, delicate project. On day one, I quickly identified that the CEO who had stepped down was short of skills and ability to run the head office of this organization. The brand and business growth were well-driven by the board's strategic planning, however, the organizational elements and infrastructure were in need of everything that I would normally recommend for a startup business. By the end of week two, 99% of the team had resigned and I was working alongside the President and Board as the interim CEO to bring the operation into alignment with what it needed to support the organization's immediate needs and considered forecasted growth.

In six months, I had recruited a new team and put in place systems and processes. The business was working more fluidly and less-reactively, and could further flourish with integrity. I was then able to hand the reins over to a long-term Chief Executive Officer so he could further develop the business and personalize the foundations laid.

This is one example of the interesting scenarios I have encountered over the past few decades.

SYNOPSIS SNAPSHOT

- Allow for the shifts
- Continue with all the teachings
- Continue to read your goals
- Visualize daily

Nearly all men

can stand adversity,

but if you want

to test a man's character,

give him power.

~Abraham Lincoln

Image sourced from quotesvalley

Scientific research has demonstrated only a 0.1% difference between the genetic make-up of all humans. So, at the level of high-performance, the tiniest of shifts in perspective play a huge role in distinguishing the highest of achievers in all areas.

These tiny shifts in perspective have the biggest impact for those like you who are already achieving and creating close to or at world-class levels.

Coaching is powerful and impactful. And I help my clients make these tiny shifts that equate to big change.

"*Perfection is not attainable, but we can catch excellence*"

VINCE LOMBARDI
(C. 1913–1970)
ITALIAN AMERICAN FOOTBALLER
COACH AND EXECUTIVE IN THE NATIONAL
FOOTBALL LEAGUE

Vince Lombardi (Head Coach) with Green Bay Packers quarterback Bart Starr. Image sourced from Wikipedia

DAYS 22 – 28 OPTIONAL READING

FOR OPTIMIZATION

At this stage, evaluating and optimizing the strategic plan during the re-launch of the business is our priority. It is important to ensure that operations are heading in a unified direction and that employees are motivated and aligned with business expectations.

Our role is to highlight successful outcomes to management and recommend improvements in areas not yet affected. Cooperation and resilience are the capstones to successful business. A periodic review will monitor activities and efficiency within your organization.

Bear in mind, business transformation is not easy—it is a highly complex process, and many transformations fail. Transformation efforts are more likely to succeed if you follow these guidelines:

- Approach transformation as a continuous exercise with focused management and teams (i.e. not as a 'once and done' event);

- Develop a simple narrative to support the complexity;
- Take a minimally viable approach to evolving business models;
- Focus on adapting capabilities;
- Invest in new products and services; and
- Divest in products and services that are non-strategic

In this stage of the program, we must focus on gaining freedom and flexibility in the market.

At this point, the company has gained confidence and aligned its business target with organizational performance. Further operational changes could increase market share and improve competition in the market. Often, businesses require an IPO (Initial Public Offering) merger and acquisition steps that enrich their presence and their relevance in the industry.

Congratulations! You have mastered your new mindset, adapted your goals, now with clarity and confidence you are able to start thinking about the next step and optimization towards meeting your objectives and succession plan.

Over the next seven days, reflect on your achievements over the past 21 days and start focusing on optimizing your personal and professional life and your business toward your objectives.

Your first point of focus is to establish your team so you can delegate as much of what you don't need to do or don't want to do to people you can trust and who have the skills to complete those tasks as well or better than you. This will help you retain clarity around your newly adapted alignment, so you can focus on growth.

It is now imperative to set up weekly operation reports, so that key team members from each department can report to you regularly and help keep your finger on the pulse across all departments.

Aim to be in a position where smooth business operation is not reliant on you each day to function. If you are not already past this milestone, once the business reaches a point where it operates fluidly—lean and agile without you—well done! You have run a business with a sustainable model that can be sold at a greater price, be duplicated or, if it's your own business, retained for an income while you take quality time to focus on other projects, holidays, and family.

Once you have delegated tasks, review the checklist noted below. I developed this diagram to give my clients a snapshot of a business that is optimized and ready to meet the next milestone.

EXTRA HOME PLAY
AT THE ACADEMY OF BUSINESS

Log onto Academy of Business/Optimization to access the following templates to aid further success:

• Optimization Checklist

Online templates are updated regularly.

Below you will find the Optimization Checklist used at the time of writing this book.

OPTIMIZATION CHECKLIST

✔ Surround yourself with like-minded people

✔ If things change environmentally, be mindful and flexible to adapt your goals and path to meet your greatest goals, which are aligned with purpose

✔ Educate yourself through good conversations and reading positive article and books

✔ Stay innovative

✔ Put yourself first to be able to serve others for the greater good

✔ Remain calm and flexible, working with clarity and confidence. (These are fundamental ingredients shared by many successful leaders who have pushed through the trickiest of business scenarios to make the best decision for their organization at any given time)

✔ Maintain balance

✔ Value choice and freedom

✔ Strive for agility and quality, free time

✔ Aim for a Lean business to create better profit margins

✔ Aim for clarity and confidence in the business operation and in you, the driver and leader

✔ Plan a scalable business—to scale, you don't build the business, you develop the people

✔ Be systematic in your approach

✔ Prioritize dynamic integration

✔ Greater purpose

✔ Develop partnerships

✔ Grow in self-awareness

✔ Focus on alignment across all aspects of your business and life

✔ Enlist the support of a mentor

✔ Set up your business for growth

✔ Be flexible

✔ Give back

"I never did anything worth doing by accident, nor did any of my inventions come indirectly through accident, except the phonograph. No, when I have fully decided that a result is worth getting, I go about it, and make trial after trial, until it comes"

THOMAS EDISON
(C. 1847–1931)
AMERICAN INNOVATOR
CONSIDERED ONE OF AMERICA'S LEADING BUSINESSMEN

THANK YOU

I sincerely hope the contents of this handbook have helped you and anybody you share it with to establish a grounding foundation to become the best version of yourself. Continue to grow your business with purpose-driven goals aligned throughout all areas of your life.

A big thank you for your commitment, and congratulations on making it through your 28-Day journey. I wish for you the very best in success.

It has been a true honor to be part of your journey.

If you have a special success story you would like to share, I would be delighted to hear from you. You can email me at:

adriana@consultingaustralia.com.au

What next?

Take action, continue with your daily rituals and learnings, which you can personalize and build from. I recommend you revisit this handbook whenever you need it, at least every 12 months. Set aside time each year, on your birthday, New Year's Day, or perhaps before the new financial year to continue focusing your actions and compounding results to your further success.

*"My definition of success?
The more you're actively
and practically engaged, the
more successful you will feel"*

SIR RICHARD BRANSON
FOUNDER OF THE VIRGIN GROUP,
WHICH CONTROLS MORE THAN 400 COMPANIES

*Sir Richard Branson with Alberto Hazan in June 2007 helping launch
Virgin Radio Italia.
Sourced from Wikipedia*

*Joe Kornik of Consulting Magazine New York, presenting
Adriana Cecere with recognition as a Global Leader
in London Piccadilly, 7th December 2017.*

"*I never dreamed about success, I worked for it*"

ESTÉE LAUDER
(c. 1908–2004)
BORN IN QUEENS, NEW YORK
BEAUTICIAN
FOUNDER OF ESTEE LAUDER, MAC COSMETICS
AND CLINIQUE

Estée Lauder with a customer (1966). Sourced from Wikipedia.